joyful mind

A PRACTICAL GUIDE TO BUDDHIST MEDITATION

If you have a serious injury or illness, consult a health professional before practicing yoga. Not all exercises and poses are suitable for everyone, and this or any exercise program could result in injury. To reduce the risk of injury, do not force or strain. Pregnant women are advised not to practice twisting poses or any exercise that places strain on the abdomen. Women who are menstruating are advised not to practice inverted poses or poses that place heavy pressure on the abdomen. When in doubt, always consult a competent health professional.

Mention of specific companies, organizations, or authorities in this book does not imply endorsement by the publisher, nor does mention of specific companies, organizations, or authorities in the book imply that they endorse the book. Internet addresses and telephone numbers given in this book were accurate at the time the book went to press.

© 2002 by Susan Piver for Padma Projects, www.padmaprojects.com
Photographs © Susie Cushner Photography
Design: Melanie Lowe, M Space Design

All rights reserved. No part of this publication may be reproduced or transmitted in any form or by any means, electronic or mechanical, including photocopying, recording, or any other information storage and retrieval system, without the written permission of the publisher.

Printed in China
Rodale Inc. makes every effort to use ∞ acid-free ♺ recycled paper.
ISBN: 1-57954-608-0

Distributed to the book trade by St. Martin's Press

2 4 6 8 10 9 7 5 3 1   hardcover
Visit us at www.rodalestore.com, or call toll-free at (800) 848-4735.

WE **INSPIRE** AND **ENABLE** PEOPLE TO IMPROVE
THEIR LIVES AND THE WORLD AROUND THEM

thank you

Lisa Andruscavage, Josh Baran, Emily Bower, Duncan Browne, Mark Butler, Michael Carroll, Susie Cushner, Kath Delaney, Steve Gorn, Stephen Jarvis, Jennifer Kushnier, Adam Lobel, Melanie Lowe, Melvin McCloud, Berkley McKeever, William McKeever, David Nichtern, Joan Duncan Oliver, Dave O'Neal, Amy Rhodes, Rick Rowe, Kelly Schmidt, Emily Sell, Tami Simon, Eden Steinberg, Stephanie Tade, Andrew Weil, Joanna Williams, and all the remarkable teachers who share their Joyful Minds.

Produced and compiled by Susan Piver

we shall not cease from exploration
and the end of all our exploring
will be to arrive where we started
and know the place for the first time.

– t. s. eliot, "little gidding"

Welcome to *Joyful Mind*. This book contains an introduction to a variety of forms of meditation plus two compact discs.

Each practice featured herein is grounded in a lineage that is thousands of years old. From the calming practice of basic breath awareness to a powerful healing visualization technique, *Joyful Mind* offers you a chance to sample what you may have only read about, until now.

In this book, world-renowned teachers write about the style they have mastered. We invite you to go further by actually trying these practices for yourself: The first CD features one 10-minute practice from each teacher. These are the same practices you would learn if you were to visit the Buddhist meditation hall in your town or an ancient monastery in Tibet. From Tibet to Japan, from Korea to California, meditators the world over are

doing these very practices. As a special addition to these meditations, we include yoga poses designed to prepare the body for sitting.

The second CD is a gorgeous all-music disc from bansuri flute virtuoso Steve Gorn. He has performed Indian classical music all over the world and studied with the late bansuri master, Sri Gour Goswami of Calcutta. A Buddhist practitioner himself, Steve's music has deeply meditative qualities. Play this CD whenever you want to create a mood of relaxation or peace.

We invite you to sample these practices in any order that feels right to you. You may listen to them all at once or try one a week. Let your mind and heart wander through and resonate with these extraordinary practices. Let them be a gift. Welcome home.

contents

introduction

Meditation is the noble act of making friends with yourself. Breath by breath, moment by moment, we begin to learn who we really are. At first, this prospect may be interesting, shocking, appalling, mysterious, or boring. Eventually, the chop of discursive mind softens, and we find natural attunement with ourselves. We breathe in and out. We notice the play of light and dark. Sensations rise and fall in the body and in the mind. Slowly, our thoughts begin to settle, and we find that we are actually living in a very open and spacious world. We see that meditation need not be an unusual ascetic practice or even a particularly spiritual one. It is quite ordinary, yet somehow changes everything. We have just taken our seat, right in the middle of our lives.

Meditation is often associated with Buddhism, and the practices contained in *Joyful Mind* stem from Buddhist tradition. The Buddha, or "Awakened One," discovered a fundamental truth about being alive: There is no need to be anything other than who we are already. In fact, the core teaching of the Buddha is the importance of discovering who we really are. Meditation is a way of making this discovery.

Through meditation practice, we befriend our fear, craziness, desire, shame, and dullness: those things that keep us from waking up to our natural state. It is in fact our birthright to be truly alive, awake, and courageous.

The Buddha didn't make up meditation; it has been practiced in one form or another for many thousands of years. Therefore, it's not necessary to even think about becoming a Buddhist in order to practice meditation, just as it's not required to become a Christian to practice charity. These things are simply our natural heritage, the ground of being human.

Over the thousands of years that human beings have practiced meditation, certain specific forms have arisen that are particularly uplifting, helpful, and inspiring. Some of these are presented in *Joyful Mind*.

An unprecedented number of people are now interested in learning meditation. These practices and the philosophy behind them have irrevocably made their way West. Principles associated with meditation such as mindfulness, equanimity, and compassion are being embraced by executives as productivity tools, filmmakers as good storylines, and advertisers as ways to sell products. Our interest in these practices is at an all-time high—and so is the opportunity for confusion. Therefore, it's important to turn to authentic teachers for guidance.

We may be thinking that meditation would probably be a good thing for us but aren't sure how to begin or what to begin with. We may be asking questions like, "How many kinds of meditation are there and which one is best for me?" "Will I have to sit on the floor or in an otherwise uncomfortable position?" "Do I have to do a formal practice, or can I just make something up?" "How will I know if I'm doing it right?" In the pages that follow,

some of the most respected and beloved teachers in the world answer these questions and offer us instruction. We are invited to do more than simply read about various styles of meditation; we're actually given the opportunity to try them out. At some point, one practice may "speak" to us more than the others. In this case, a list of resources and referrals has been provided, including places to visit to discover more about a certain teaching or teacher.

The first practice, *Shamatha*, is taught by Sakyong Mipham Rinpoche, lineage-holder of the Shambhala Buddhist tradition. Shamatha, or "calm abiding," is the most basic meditation practice of all: simply sitting and placing our awareness on our breath. Shamatha alone can be a powerful lifelong practice and can serve as the root for developing other practices.

Vipassana, or "insight meditation," is said to naturally arise from Shamatha. In Vipassana, awareness is no longer placed exclusively on the breath but is allowed to rest on whatever sensations, thoughts, or feelings may arise. Larry Rosenberg, a teacher, author, former University professor, and longtime Zen and Vipassana practitioner, leads us through this practice.

Edward Espe Brown, ordained a Zen priest in 1971 by Shunryu Suzuki Roshi, teaches us *zazen*, "sitting Zen." He is also a world-famous cook and author of a number of vegetarian cookbooks.

The next practice presented in *Joyful Mind* is called *Metta*, or "Lovingkindness." Metta is the practice of generating compassion for all living beings, including oneself. It is taught by Sharon Salzberg, who is a co-founder of the world-renowned Insight Meditation Society and the Barre Center for Buddhist Studies.

Tonglen, or "sending and taking" in English, works directly with our confused tendency to focus on ourselves alone. This ancient Tibetan practice, going back to A.D. 1045, exposes the depth of our self-absorption and begins to unravel it. It is a practice specifically designed to remove obstacles that stand in the way of our natural impulse toward kindness. Here, Tonglen is taught by Acharya Judith Lief, a Buddhist teacher, writer, and student of renowned meditation master, Chögyam Trungpa Rinpoche.

Tulku Thondup offers us an extraordinary meditation on healing, whether our ailment is physical or emotional. Born in Tibet, he is a widely renowned Lama and the author of numerous Buddhist books and translations. Recognized as the reincarnation of the great Dzogchen Abbot Lushul Khenpo, he has taught at Harvard University and resides in Cambridge, Massachusetts.

In addition to these meditation teachings, also included are basic yoga postures to prepare the body for seated meditation.

Yoga and meditation are natural allies, and practicing one is a very good support for the other. Here, Cyndi Lee, yoga teacher and founder of New York City's OM yoga center, offers instruction on both preparing the body for sitting and, as important, closing your meditation practice with *Savasana*, "relaxation" that can help integrate the fruits of meditation practice.

It is our sincere hope that these teachings will bring you happiness, freedom from suffering, equanimity, joy, and the motivation to help others.

Although each of the practices included here is a different way to meditate, there is one aspect in common: taking a good posture. This doesn't mean sitting up perfectly straight without moving, as we may have been taught in elementary school. It does mean finding a way to sit up straight that is both upright and relaxed. Zen teacher Suzuki Roshi has said that taking this posture correctly is the same thing as enlightenment. That's pretty cool.

Meditation practice begins by sitting down, either cross-legged on a cushion or on a chair or bed with both feet placed firmly on the ground. It's not at all important that you be able to sit cross-legged or in any way you find uncomfortable. Sitting on a chair is just as good as sitting in full lotus position on the floor. (Really.) The important thing is to take your seat with dignity and simplicity. Then, even just sitting down to begin meditation can be an uplifting, encouraging experience.

Next, make sure your back is straight, like a tree: Trees move and sway in response to the wind, a flock of birds flying by, the sudden appearance of a rainstorm. Still, the tree points up with its branches and down with its roots. It is unmoving and moving at the same time. Feel the crown of your head reaching up to the sky while your sitting bones reach down, maybe even to the center of the earth. This way, you are said to be joining heaven and earth simply by being a human being who is sitting down.

If you are sitting on a cushion, cross your legs loosely in front of you. One leg can be in front of the other, or you can rest one ankle just above the other. Your knees should be on the ground or supported by pillows. It is enormously helpful to have your hips higher than your knees. To do this, you might need to use two or three cushions. Once your hips are higher, knees more naturally fall to the ground, making a triangle with your sitting bones. This can be very supportive.

Your hands can rest comfortably on your thighs. It's also fine to rest one hand within the other, left within right, thumb tips gently touching. This hand posture is associated with Zen, but you may just find it more comfortable.

You can keep your eyes slightly open, gazing on the floor 4 to 6 feet in front of you. Your eyes are seeing but not looking. Alternatively, feel free to simply close your eyes.

Your jaw is relaxed, chin level with the ground, tip of the tongue resting lightly behind the upper teeth. Try and keep your shoulders relaxed.

Then, as you sit with a good posture, begin to pay attention to your breath. Place your attention on the breath, either at your nostrils or abdomen. Your breath is always in the present moment; it can't be otherwise. So the simplest way to "be present" is to be with your breath.

Sitting in this way is the basis for all the meditation practices that are to follow.

shamatha

BY SAKYONG MIPHAM RINPOCHE

The untrained mind is like a wild horse. It runs away when we try to find it, shies when we try to approach it. If we find a way to ride it, it takes off with the bit in its teeth and finally throws us right into the mud. There is potential for communication and rapport between horse and rider, between mind and self, but the horse needs to be trained to be a willing participant in that relationship.

We train our minds with *shamatha* practice, the most simple form of sitting meditation. Shamatha is a Sanskrit word that means "peacefully abiding." Like all types of meditation, it rests upon two basic principles, known in Tibetan as *ngotro* and *gom*. Ngotro refers to "being introduced" to the object of meditation, while gom is "becoming familiar." In shamatha practice, we are introduced to and become familiar with the simple act of breathing. This is our object of concentration, the place we return to again and again when the mind has run off and we find ourselves clutching the horse's neck, hoping we won't end up too far from home.

Why Practice Shamatha?

Meditation is based on the premise that the natural state of the mind is calm and clear. It provides a way to train our mind to settle into this state. Our first reason for meditating might be that we want some freedom from our agitated mind. We want to discover the basic goodness of our natural mind.

To do this requires us first to slow down and experience our mind as it is. In the process, we get to know how our mind works. We see that wherever the mind is abiding—in anger, in desire, in jealousy, or in peace—that is where we also are abiding. We begin to see that we have a choice in the matter: We do not have to act on the whim of every thought. We can abide peacefully. Meditation is a way to slow down and see how our mind works.

The untrained mind is weak and inflexible. It lives in a zone of comfort. When the boundaries of that zone are challenged, it reacts by becoming more rigid. In contrast, the trained mind is strong, flexible, and workable. Because it can stretch beyond where it feels comfortable, it's responsive—not reactive—to challenges. Through shamatha, we can train our mind to be flexible and tuned in to what's happening now. We can apply this workable mind in all aspects of our lives including our livelihood, our relationships, and our spiritual path. So another reason to meditate is to develop a strong, supple mind that we can put to work.

It's easy to associate meditation with spirituality because when we experience a moment of peacefully abiding, it seems so far out. Our mind is no longer drifting, thinking about a million things. The sun comes up or a beautiful breeze comes along, and all of a sudden we feel the breeze and we are completely in tune. We think, "That's a very spiritual experience! It's a religious experience! At least worth a poem or a letter home." Yet all that's happening is that for a moment we are in tune with our mind. Our mind is present and harmonious. Before, we were so busy and bewildered that we didn't even notice the breeze. Our mind couldn't even stay put long enough to watch the sun come up, which takes 2½ minutes. Now we can keep it in one place long enough to acknowledge and appreciate our surroundings. Now we are really here. This has nothing to do with religion or a spiritual path. It has everything to do with simply being human.

Preparing to Practice

The basic premise of shamatha meditation is "not too tight, not too loose." This holds true in every aspect of the practice—finding the right environment, preparing our body and mind to meditate, holding our posture, noticing thoughts and emotions, and bringing our mind back to the breath. The instructions are very clear, and we should follow them as precisely as possible. Some gentleness is also necessary, or else meditation becomes a way in which we're trying to measure up against a hopeless ideal. It's important not to expect perfection or get hooked on the finer points of the instruction. The practice takes consistent effort, and it can also be joyful.

One of the simple things that we can do is to create a good environment for practice—a place that is comfortable, quiet, and clean. A corner of your room that feels uplifted and spacious and private is a good enough place. It's unproductive to get caught up in chasing your idea of the perfect place to meditate. Some people from the city will go into the mountains to meditate in peace and find that the crickets and the birds won't shut up!

Timing is also important. Decide on a regular time to practice each day and try to stick with it. A 10-minute period in the morning is a good place to begin. The more consistent you can be in keeping to the routine, the better.

Planning is another element. It's better not to just sit down and hope for the best. If you plop down on your seat straight from the office or right after an argument, you may spend the whole session trying to slow down enough even to remember that you're meditating. If you're agitated, a slow walk might be in order. If you're drowsy, a cool shower before beginning the session might help. It can be inspiring to read a little about meditation first as a reminder of why you're practicing. Working with yourself in ways like this is intelligent and honest and can create the proper mind and body for good practice. But remember, preparation is not meditation; it is just preparation.

Half the challenge of meditation is simply getting to your seat. At the beginning of a session, you may suddenly discover that you have more important things to do—housework to do or phone calls to make or e-mails to write. One way to work with this kind of procrastination is to build a routine around preliminary stretching or walking before your session. This gives you a way to ease into it by softening your body and mind before you begin meditating. The more regularly you practice the better you'll get at working with the strategies that the untrained mind cooks up to keep you from making it to your seat.

Taking Your Seat

You can use different postures for meditation, but under ordinary circumstances, sitting is best. Whether you're sitting in a chair or on a cushion, consider the meditation seat your throne—the center of your practice and your life.

When you sit down, take a balanced, grounded posture to allow the energy in the center of your body to move freely. If you're on a cushion, sit with your legs loosely crossed. If you're in a chair, keep your legs uncrossed and your feet flat on the floor. Imagine that a string attached to the top of your head is pulling you upright. Let your body settle around your erect spine. Place your hands on your thighs, in a place not so far forward that it begins to pull your shoulders down, nor so far back that your shoulders contract and pinch the spine. The fingers are close and relaxed—not spread out in a grip, as if you can't let yourself go.

having a mind that is at peace with itself,
a mind that is clear and joyous,
is the basis of happiness and compassion.

Tuck your chin in and relax your jaw. The tongue is also relaxed, resting against your upper teeth. Your mouth is ever so slightly open. Your gaze is downward, with the eyelids almost half-shut. The eyes aren't looking; the eyes just see. It is the same with sound: We aren't listening, but we do hear. In other words, we're not focusing with our senses.

Slouching impairs your breathing, which directly affects the mind. If you slump, you'll be struggling with your body at the same time that you're trying to train your mind. What you want to be doing is the opposite: synchronizing your body and mind. When your focus is wavering, check your posture. Bring yourself back to the upright position. Imagine the string pulling your spine up straight, and relax your body around it.

Working with the Breath

Our mind usually jumps wildly from thought to thought. We replay the past; we fantasize about the future. In meditation, we place our mind on an object and keep it there. In shamatha meditation, the object is the simple act of breathing. The breath represents being alive in the immediacy of the moment.

Using breathing as the object of meditation is especially good for calming a busy mind. The steady flow of the breath soothes the mind and allows for steadiness and relaxation. This is ordinary breathing; nothing is exaggerated. One simple technique is to count the in- and out-cycles of breathing from one to 21. We breathe in and then out—one. In and then out—two. Place your mind on the breathing and count each cycle of breath.

Gathering the Mind

As you focus on the breath, you'll notice that various thoughts and emotions arise. When this happens, acknowledge that you are thinking and return your focus to the breath. In focusing, you are bringing yourself back to attention. You are centering yourself in your mind and placing that mind on the breath. You are slowly settling. You're gradually slowing the mind. When you first begin to do this, the movement of thoughts may feel like a rushing waterfall. But as you continue to apply the technique of recognizing thoughts and returning your focus to the breath, the torrent slows down to a river, then to a meandering stream, which eventually flows into a deep, calm ocean.

For the movement of the mind to slow down like this takes long, consistent practice. A good practice is one that we keep doing 10 minutes a day, year after year. Through ups and through downs, slowly we become familiar with the natural stability, strength, and clarity of the mind. It becomes natural to return to that place. We let go of our conceptual ideas about

it. We can relax there and enjoy it. We begin to let this natural state of basic goodness infuse our entire lives.

Meditation practice predates Buddhism and all of the world religions. It has lasted through the centuries because it is direct, potent, and effective. If meditation becomes part of your life, please consider seeking further instruction from an experienced meditator. It might also be helpful to become part of a community of practitioners.

I have learned these instructions from my teachers and am glad to pass them on to you. May these instructions bring natural calm abiding into your life. Having a mind that is at peace with itself, a mind that is clear and joyous, is the basis of happiness and compassion.

SAKYONG MIPHAM RINPOCHE

Sakyong Mipham Rinpoche is the leader of the international Shambhala community and holder of the Shambhala Buddhist meditation lineage of his father, the late Chögyam Trungpa Rinpoche. The Sakyong is recognized as the incarnation of the great 19th-century Tibetan Buddhist teacher Mipham Rinpoche.

vipassana

BY LARRY ROSENBERG

I would like to share with you a two-part meditation. The first part is called *Anapanasati*, which in the ancient Pali language of India means "breath awareness." It goes back about 2,600 years and was used by the Buddha to attain enlightenment. I learned it from Indian, Burmese, Thai, and Vietnamese teachers in Asia. The second part is called *Vipassana* or "insight meditation." Anapanasati and Vipassana have been practiced together for thousands of years; Anapanasati naturally and easily gives rise to Vipassana. The first practice calms the mind by focusing on breath. In the second practice, we release focus on breath alone to focus on whatever arises.

The Buddha taught that there is so much unnecessary suffering in life because we don't understand ourselves very well. Would you like to get to know yourself? If so, sit down and take a look! Breath awareness is a way to do just this. Conscious breathing helps to calm and stabilize the mind so that it is fit to see into and understand itself.

To begin with, it's important to establish the body in a position or posture that's both comfortable and stable. Whether you're in a chair or kneeling on a bench or sitting on a cushion cross-legged, it is helpful for the body to be erect so that the head, neck, and spine are in a straight line with the chin tilted down just ever so slightly. Good posture helps the body breathe properly and the mind stay alert.

Next, it's important to inhabit the body with awareness. Be sensitive to the fact that you're sitting. See if there is any obvious tension in the body. Common places where tensions accumulate for many of us would be the jaw, rather tight because we're determined. The shoulders may be hunched up, posed for action. Take just a few moments and move through the body with mindfulness, noticing any area that's contracted or tight, and, just for a moment or so, touch this area of the body with awareness. Probably it will relax a bit. It will soften.

You can keep the eyes closed with the lids fully shut or half-open without trying to see anything in particular. Put your hands on your knees or thighs, or clasp one hand inside the other.

Now you are ready to start observing the breath. It is helpful to take three or four deep breaths, a little bit deeper than your normal breathing. Then allow the breathing to assume its own rhythm. Let it flow naturally. You can rest your attention on the air coming in and out of the nostrils or on the rise and fall of the abdomen. Station your attention at either one, and watch each breath as it goes in and out.

Take it one breath at a time, giving full care and attention to each in breath and each out breath in turn, staying awake during the pause between breaths. Learn to allow the breathing to unfold naturally. If you find that you direct the breath— and most of us do at the beginning— simply observe this tendency to control. Such mindfulness will restore the natural flow of the breathing. This practice is not about attaining some special kind of breathing. It is not a yoga breathing exercise or breath therapy. It is an awareness practice, and what we are aware of is the sensation of breathing exactly as it is. You might find yourself straining or struggling. Notice that. When you do, the energy usually smoothes out.

As you practice, you'll find that from time to time you're not attentive to the breath at all. You have some other preoccupation about the past or the future. Perhaps you will get caught up in sounds or bodily sensations. As soon as you see that you are not in contact with the breath, very gently, very gracefully ease back to the in- and out-breath once again. This coming back to the breath is without judgment, without blame, without finding fault. It's just coming back. It's important that you do this with gentleness because, as you begin to learn this method, you may have to do it a fair amount. If you practice, it gets easier. Attention to breathing will become continuous.

As the mind begins to calm down, it is fit to open up the second aspect of our practice, what is called Vipassana or insight meditation. Insight meditation is a deep seeing into the nature of the whole mind-body process. It is a first-hand, direct way of coming to know ourselves as we truly are. In the Buddha's teaching, it is this clear seeing that liberates us from the suffering that we go through unnecessarily. In this next mode of practice, we retain focus on the breath as part of our method, but we loosen our grip a bit. Earlier, we were developing calm by attending to the breath exclusively; everything other than breath was considered a distraction. Now the breath sensations are not the sole object of focus. Now, we experience the breath as an anchor, helping us remain fully alert to our experience.

insight meditation is the practice of liberation: by making friends with our old wounds, fears, anger, and loneliness, we free ourselves.

In Vipassana, we learn to fully receive our experience—whatever it is—in an intimate and unbiased way. Just to sit, breathe, be ourselves, and see what is there. Nothing particular is "supposed" to happen. Whatever is happening is perfect. We learn to observe our experience without holding on to what we like or pushing away what we don't like. Thoughts, moods, emotions will come and go. The body will feel a certain way; these feelings will come and go as well. The same will be true of sounds and smells. What aspect of all this do you attend to? Let life tell you! Different elements of the process of mind and body will be distinctive, strong, vivid. They will naturally capture your attention. The challenge is to open to experience exactly as it is, with mindfulness. All the while, conscious breathing will accompany and support you like a good friend.

In this second mode of practice, unlike in Anapanasati, nothing is a distraction! Whatever we encounter is our life at that moment, and that is what we learn to be mindful of. Sensations will arise in the body. The practice is simply to bring awareness to those sensations. Can you become sensitive to bodily life without judging it? Not condemning what you don't like, not grasping on to what you do like. Sometimes the body will feel wonderful, meditative calm permeating the body with a wonderfully relaxed feeling. Can you let that happen without grasping it and trying to keep it forever? If you can't, you'll find that you suffer. See if that's true. Test it.

The same attitude applies to the mind. And when I say mind, I mean thoughts, images, and emotions—the different moods we go through, the likes and dislikes and fears and loves and loneliness that make up human existence. The mind grasps after things, holding them tightly or pushing them away aggressively. Sometimes the mind is confused, feels covered in darkness, is ambivalent and unresolved. At other times, it feels very fresh and clear. Can you let whatever is happening happen without preferring one state of mind over the other?

Insight meditation is the practice of liberation: By making friends with our old wounds, fears, anger, and loneliness, we free ourselves.

Just relax, breathe, and know what's there. Whatever is in you starts to present itself. This way of attending to your experience, watching its nature from moment to moment, from breath to breath, takes us to another dimension of consciousness, one which is spacious and silent. The silent mind is tremendously fulfilling. It is highly charged with life and touches the human heart deeply. You may find that you are wiser and kinder! Anyone who has tasted this emptiness no longer needs teachers or books to know its value.

Now it is important to learn how to work back and forth between these two modes of practice, calm and insight. As you're able to do so, sit and enjoy the show. Let it all happen and stay awake in the midst of it. Be intimate with your experience. From time to time, as you find yourself caught up in thoughts, starting to analyze and psychologize, as the mind loses focus and gets lost in its own content, simply go back to the breath as an exclusive object of attention. Fine-tune your attention with simple breath awareness and either conclude the session that way or, if you feel your mind has calmed down, once again open the field to include whatever is there. It's sort of the right and left hand working together, helping to bring us to understanding and love.

Finally, a brief suggestion about a large subject: meditation in daily life. The Buddha's teachings are not limited to silent sitting meditation. We are encouraged to bring the mindfulness we develop while sitting to all of the activities that make up our lives. Bring undivided, full attention to every situation. If you are washing the dishes, wash the dishes. Notice if you get lost in thoughts about the past or future, thoughts that separate you from intimate contact with the activity of washing dishes. If you find yourself distracted, simply return to what you are actually doing. This suggestion applies to everything we encounter in our daily lives: eating, driving, working, waking up, and going to sleep. Nothing is left out. Start paying attention to how you actually live. Bringing alertness to daily life strengthens sitting meditation; sitting meditation enhances our sensitivity to daily life. Many of us have found this constant alternating between quiet contemplation and mindful action a beautiful way to live.

LARRY ROSENBERG

Larry Rosenberg practiced Zen in Korea and Japan before coming to Vipassana. He is the founder and a guiding teacher at the Cambridge Insight Meditation Center. Larry is also a guiding teacher at the Insight Meditation Society in Barre, Massachusetts. He is the author of two books about meditation.

z a z e n

BY EDWARD ESPE BROWN

The meditation I offer is called *zazen* in Japanese. Introduced into Japan by Zen Master Eihei Dogen in the 13th century, it is from the Soto Zen tradition.

Zen practice is often associated with either koans or sitting meditation. In the Soto tradition, rather than using koans— "What was your original face before your parents were born?"—we emphasize the posture and presence of zazen. In zazen, you sit down and spend time with yourself. You are not getting anything done or consuming anything. You are given a few basic pieces of advice, primarily about posture, and are encouraged to find out for yourself how

to continue sitting. It's that simple—and that difficult.

The essentials are rather straightforward: Sit down and be quiet, find a way to sit up straight with fullness of spirit, and keep at it. Many things will happen. Let them. Zen suggests that the point is to experience your experience, rather than seeking to control it.

So whether it is on the floor using some cushions of your choosing, or in a chair, see if you can find some way to sit up straight without slumping, without leaning against anything. Study how to be balanced left to right and front to back. You are like a tree, growing to the heavens. See if you can find a balance between the effort needed to sit up straight, and ease, the softness of mind and body associated with absorption.

We simply say, "Take your best posture." Because the body is a physical manifestation of consciousness, working on your posture is a direct, immediate way to work on your attitude, to work on your mind. You are allowing your body and mind to open, your vitality—chi and energy—to flow freely. You are "unfolding." You are meeting life with the fullness of your presence. Rather than ducking or dodging, taking (unconsciously) the posture you (implicitly) believe is to your best advantage, you go ahead and embody the fullness of your body, of your being. You are "liberated" from your story. You are not so easily knocked over by life when you take this posture.

You will have many ideas about what meditation is supposed to be, and your experience in meditation will not match your ideas. You will believe that the important point is to get your experience to match your ideas of what your experience should be like. When you are unable to do this, you will say that meditation is difficult. You will be ready to give up. But when you can "just sit," having the experience you have, whatever it is, without comparing it to what it should be, you will have true ease. No longer busy chasing after some imagined perfection, you rest in the moment. You "own" your body and mind. In Zen this is called, "No more worry about not being perfect." Welcome to being you.

Eventually, soon enough really, you will realize that what you are doing is maybe, possibly, probably not nearly as important as the way you do it, and you will start to consider whether there is some way to settle in, to settle down, to live the love you have in your heart, and make it real in

when you can "just sit," having the
experience you have, whatever it is,
without comparing it to what it should be,
you will have true ease.

your life. Is there some way to be at home in this being I find myself being? To be at home in this body and this mind?

If you go to a Zen center, you may find that the forms of practice are presented quite strictly, but in the context of your own life, you can decide how strictly to do "formal" practice. You can also find many ways to simply "stop" in the midst of your life. For instance, I often do "coffee meditation" in the mornings, bringing a cup of coffee with me to my meditation cushion. While I sit quietly, from time to time I take a sip of coffee and thoroughly enjoy its robust fragrance and flavor. Similarly, you may find various places and times to sit quietly, gathering yourself together.

At the same time most people find that for meditation to have a significant impact on their lives, they need to make a commitment to a regular practice of sitting, whether it is at home, at a meditation center, or with a group of friends. You might find that sitting with others is inspiring and supportive.

You might be drawn to meditating first thing in the morning, or inspired to spend a few minutes sitting quietly before bed. Additionally there are dozens of resources that present instructions you might find useful (including those in this CD/book). Go ahead. Try things out. See for yourself what fits with your life and engages your being. See for yourself what matters to you most deeply and if meditation of some sort helps you connect with what matters most.

After 20 years of practice at the Zen Center of San Francisco where I became a disciple of Shunryu Suzuki Roshi—and more than 15 years of practice since then—I have continued to find it useful to spend at least a few minutes sitting quietly each morning. Rather than worrying about how much you should practice or how perfectly you are practicing, it is more important to practice regularly. Do something you can commit to. Your life will change because you have incorporated a life change.

Imagine: The bell rings to begin the period of meditation. You sit yourself down. You simply stop, sit down, and watch as you race across the internal landscape, driven to accomplish, driven to perform. Keep watching. As you do, you allow yourself to breathe, to notice you are breathing, and, suddenly, you are at rest. You've come to rest at the same time you are sitting with someone very busy figuring, analyzing, judging, aiming, progressing now forward, now back, and never arriving.

Finally it's okay to catch your breath.

EDWARD ESPE BROWN

Edward Espe Brown began cooking and practicing Zen in 1965 and was ordained as a priest by Shunryu Suzuki Roshi in 1971. He has been head resident teacher at each of the San Francisco Zen Centers—Tassajara, Green Gulch, and City Center—and has led meditation retreats and cooking classes throughout the United States as well as in Austria, Germany, Spain, and England. He is the author of several acclaimed cookbooks.

Ed was the first head resident cook at Tassajara Zen Mountain Center in California, from 1967 to 1970. From 1979 to 1983 he worked at the celebrated Greens Restaurant in San Francisco, serving as busboy, waiter, floor manager, wine buyer, cashier, host, and manager. He has been teaching vegetarian cooking classes since 1985.

metta

BY SHARON SALZBERG

All human beings are united by an urge for happiness. We want an experience that takes us beyond our small, separate sense of self; a feeling of being at home with ourselves and one another. At the root of even the most terrible addiction or violence lies this urge to be happy. It may be twisted or distorted by ignorance of where happiness is actually to be found — yet, that fundamental longing for genuine happiness is there.

The Pali word for lovingkindness is metta. The practice of metta helps us honor the urge toward happiness in both ourselves and others. We develop the ability to embrace all parts of ourselves: the difficult aspects as well as the noble. As we continue practicing from that base of inner generosity, metta gives us the ability to embrace all parts of the world.

Ultimately, metta overcomes the illusion of separateness. The unconditional experience of lovingkindness is a radical sense of non-separation. Thus, the nature of metta is to dissolve all the states associated with the fundamental error of separateness: fear, alienation, loneliness, despair, and feelings of fragmentation.

It's said that the Buddha first taught metta meditation as an antidote to fear. According to legend, he sent a group of monks off to meditate in a forest that was inhabited by tree spirits. The tree spirits resented the monks' presence, so they decided to scare them away. They transformed themselves into ghoulish visions, made terrible shrieking sounds, and created awful smells. The monks, appropriately terrified, fled the forest. "Please, Lord Buddha," they begged, "send us to meditate in some other forest."

The Buddha said, "I'm going to send you back to the very same forest—but this time, I'll give you the only protection you need." And so the Buddha gave the first-ever teaching of metta meditation. He encouraged the monks to recite the phrases that follow—but more important, to actually do the heartfelt practice of lovingkindness.

Like many such stories, this one has a happy ending. It's said that the monks returned to the forest and practiced metta. The tree spirits were so moved by the energy of lovingkindness they generated that they decided they quite liked the monks being there after all. They decided to serve and protect them.

Whether this parable is literally true, its inner meaning endures: A mind filled with fear can be penetrated by the quality of lovingkindness. Moreover, a mind filled with lovingkindness cannot be overcome by fear.

The beginning of metta practice is learning how to be your own friend. As the Buddha said, "You can search the entire universe for someone more deserving of your love and affection than you are yourself, but that person is not to be found anywhere. You, yourself, more than anybody in the universe, deserve your own love and affection." Very few of us embrace ourselves in this way. Metta practice is the key to this treasure. Too, loving others without any love for ourselves tramples on healthy boundaries. So you begin by sending metta to yourself. The traditional practice uses a series of phrases, as follows:

may all beings be free from danger.
may all beings be happy.
may all beings be healthy.
may all beings live with ease.

May I be free from danger.
May I be happy.
May I be healthy.
May I live with ease.

If these phrases don't touch your heart, feel free to come up with your own. The important thing is not to recite the "correct" lines, but to use words that are meaningful to you.

From here, the practice proceeds in a very structured and specific way. After directing metta to yourself, you move on to someone you find inspiring or to whom you feel grateful. This person is called "the benefactor." Bring this person's presence into your mind and direct the metta phrases to him or her:

May you be free from danger.
May you be happy.
May you be healthy.
May you live with ease.

Next, move on to a beloved friend, sending unconditional lovingkindness to that person in the same way:

May you be free from danger.
May you be happy.
May you be healthy.
May you live with ease.

The next person you go to is traditionally called "neutral." This is somebody you neither like nor dislike. If you have trouble coming up with a suitable neutral person, try thinking of a clerk you've seen at the supermarket, or perhaps someone who walks his dog past your house. Again, use the same phrases you've used before, but this time directed to the neutral person:

May you be free from danger.
May you be happy.
May you be healthy.
May you live with ease.

Now you're ready to send lovingkindness

to someone with whom you've had difficulty or conflict. To send lovingkindness to difficult or threatening people is not to forget about your own needs. It doesn't require denial of your own pain, anger, or fear. Nor does doing this practice mean you're excusing abuse or cruelty. Rather, you're engaging in the marvelous process of discovering and cultivating your inherent capacity for unconditional love. It doesn't have to do with being passive or complacent in terms of the other person; it has to do with your own spiritual expansion. Directing metta toward a difficult person leads to the discovery of your own capacity for lovingkindness that's born of freedom.

May you be free from danger.
May you be happy.
May you be healthy.
May you live with ease.

In the final phase of the practice, we move on to offer metta to all beings everywhere, without distinction or exception:

May all beings be free from danger.
May all beings be happy.
May all beings be healthy.
May all beings live with ease.

In lovingkindness, our minds are open and expansive—spacious enough to contain all the pleasures and pains of a life fully lived. Pain, in this context, doesn't feel like a betrayal or an overwhelming force. It is part of the reality of human experience and an opportunity for us to practice maintaining our authentic presence.

Every single one of us can cultivate lovingkindness and wisdom so that happiness becomes our powerful and natural expression of being.

SHARON SALZBERG

Sharon has been practicing and studying in a variety of Buddhist traditions since 1970. She has trained with teachers from many countries including India, Burma, Nepal, Bhutan, and Tibet. Since 1974, Sharon has been leading retreats worldwide. She teaches both intensive awareness practice and the profound cultivation of lovingkindness and compassion.

Sharon is a co-founder and guiding teacher of the Insight Meditation Society in Barre, Massachusetts, devoted to offering meditation training in silent retreats of various lengths. She is also a co-founder of the Barre Center for Buddhist Studies, a center that focuses on the integration of the Buddhist teachings into the modern world.

tonglen

BY ACHARYA JUDITH LIEF

When the Buddha was a young child, he led a sheltered life, brought up in a wealthy family. His father was a regional king and as such, officiated at ceremonies and state occasions. One of these annual celebrations was the planting festival, which took place when the farmers were about to sow the year's crops. It was a big event, and the local farmers and villagers would come from all around to celebrate.

At one of these planting ceremonies, when the Buddha was just a young boy, he was happily playing with his friends until he saw the plow go into the earth. As the plow cut through the soil and made a furrow, he became upset. The young Buddha was touched by how much life was disrupted and destroyed in the simple act of planting food. He saw the little bugs scurrying away from the plow and the worms cut in two. He saw lots of confused little grubs and other beings that were down below abruptly thrust to the surface and beings that used to be on the surface buried down below. As their world was flipped upside down, they seemed to be totally disoriented and unhappy. So many beings were suffering.

The Buddha was so struck by this experience that he left the festivities and sat by himself under a tree to think about what he had seen. It appeared to him that just to survive on the earth, we must inevitably cause other beings to suffer. No matter how kind we try to be, we cannot avoid it. Even the seemingly innocent act of growing food inevitably causes some beings to suffer and die.

That realization, which took place when the Buddha was just a boy, was like a seed that later ripened and inspired the Buddha to begin his personal search to understand the nature of suffering, why there is so much suffering in the world, and whether anything can be done about it. The awareness of suffering had touched his heart and awakened his kindness.

When we open ourselves to others, we are also opening ourselves to pain. As in this story of the Buddha, when we are aware of the suffering of other beings, as well as of our own suffering, kindness arises as a natural response. But we have a tendency to shield ourselves from pain and cover over that awareness. We reject those parts of our own experiences that are painful, and we also avoid facing the pain we see all around us. By distancing ourselves from pain, we distance ourselves from one another. We lose the ground of connection that makes kindness possible.

The only way to maintain that connection is to extend our awareness to include all of our experiences, not just the parts that we find comfortable. Meditation practice is a good way to begin because it is a process of becoming aware of whatever comes up in our minds, both good and bad, painful and pleasurable. We are learning to be open to who we are and whatever we are experiencing. So meditation practice is not just a mental exercise; it is a way of making friends with ourselves at a very basic level. Step by step we are learning more about ourselves and accepting and integrating those parts of ourselves we had rejected.

As we learn to accept ourselves, we are at the same time learning to accept other people. It may seem that there are always other people around and we have no choice but to accept them, unless we throw everyone out or become a hermit; but just putting up with people is not the

in tonglen practice, we are cultivating
the same tenderness of heart that
started the buddha himself on his
journey to awakening.

same as accepting them. Acceptance is the tender and gentle process of opening our hearts to others, to ourselves, and to our common ground of suffering. Kindness begins at this immediate, personal level of experience.

By cultivating an attitude of acceptance and fundamental friendliness, we can lessen not only our own fear and tension, but also that of the people around us. We can actually shift the atmosphere in the direction of relaxation and kindness and in that way be a force for healing. To the extent that we are relaxed and open ourselves, the people around us begin to pick up on it. It is like putting a drop of water on a blotter—one little drop just spreads and spreads.

We might prefer to ignore our tendencies to focus on our own concerns and ignore the concerns of others. However, if we want to cultivate kindness, we first need to understand our own selfishness. That is where we begin. We need to stop and take a good look at this fixation with ourselves.

Most of the time, we are so used to being selfish that we hardly notice it. Our self-interest is like a background noise we no longer hear. It is a constant buzzing that we cannot seem to shut off. As we go about our business we are always saying, "What's in it for me, what's in it for me?" That undertone is there whether we are robbing banks or working in intensive care. Because of it, our actions always have a twist.

With children, selfishness is more on the surface. If you ask a child to cut two pieces of cake, one for her and one for her sister, it is likely that her piece will be a little bigger—or if not bigger, it will have the icing flower on it. Clever mothers have one child cut the cake and the other one choose which of the two pieces she wants. In that way you get surgically exact cake cutting.

By the time we are grown-ups, we have been told about sharing and we know better than to let our selfishness display itself so blatantly. This does not mean it is gone, however, only that we are more sneaky. We may just put one little extra particularly yummy-looking mushroom in our rice, or we might graduate to a more advanced form of selfishness and give away the best mushroom in order to bask in how virtuous we are.

Our fixation on ourselves may not be so crude; it could be as subtle as the unquestioned assumption that we are the center and all else is the fringe. Our approach is that although other people matter, we happen to matter just a little bit more. If you look at a room full of people, chances are that each one has her little circle around her, of which she is the center and everyone else is the fringe. So everybody is looking out and checking back, looking out and checking back, each

from her own little world. It is like a game I used to play with each of my daughters in which I would say, "I'm 'me' and you're 'you.'" And she would respond, "No, I'm 'me' and you're 'you.'" Of course this game could go on and on forever, because no one would budge from their position as the center of things.

The contemplative practice called *tonglen* in Tibetan, or "sending and taking" in English, works directly with this powerful tendency to focus on ourselves. The practice of tonglen exposes the depth of our self-absorption and begins to undermine it. It is a practice specifically designed to remove that obstacle and the many other obstacles that stand in the way of our natural impulse toward kindness.

Tonglen is sometimes described as a practice of "exchanging self and other." This is because the goal of tonglen is to flip that pattern of self-absorption around completely, to the point where instead of putting ourselves first, we put others first. Tonglen practice goes from the starting point of putting ourselves first through the middle ground of viewing ourselves and others equally to the fruition of putting others before ourselves.

If our view is to focus on ourselves, then our actions will tend to feed that view by grabbing onto whatever builds us up and getting rid of whatever threatens us. Our habitual activity is to protect ourselves by constantly picking and choosing, accepting and rejecting—but in tonglen practice, once again we reverse our usual approach. Instead of taking in what we desire and rejecting what we do not, we take in what we have rejected and send out what we desire—basically the opposite of "normal." Tonglen practice completely reverses our usual way of going about things.

Why in heavens would anyone want to do tonglen? For one thing, our usual way of going about things is not all that satisfying. In tonglen, as we become more aware of the extent of our self-absorption, we realize how limited a view that is. Also, self-absorbed as we may be, we cannot help but be affected by the degree of pain and suffering in the world and want to do something about it. All around us we see people suffering and, on top of that, creating more suffering for themselves daily. But so are we! In fact, we are they—that's the whole point. The confusion we see—that's our confusion. When we see all those people suffering—that's our suffering. We cannot separate ourselves from others; it is a totally interconnected web.

In tonglen practice, we are cultivating the same tenderness of heart that started the Buddha himself on his journey to awakening. If we are losing heart, tonglen is a way of reconnecting with it. Tonglen has nothing to do with being a goody-goody or covering up our selfishness with a patina of phony niceness. The point is not to berate ourselves or force ourselves to be kinder. If we think we are not kind enough, it may not be that we are less kind than other people but that we are more honest. So tonglen begins with honesty and acceptance and goes on from there.

In the same way that it is possible to cultivate mindfulness and awareness through meditation practice, we can cultivate kindness through the practice of tonglen. Through tonglen practice we learn to work straightforwardly with the difficulties we encounter and extend ourselves more wholeheartedly to others. Tonglen is training in how to take on suffering and give out love. It is a natural complement to mindfulness practice, a natural extension of the acceptance and self-knowledge that comes as a result of sitting meditation.

Each time you practice tonglen, begin with basic mindfulness practice. It is important to take some time to let your mind settle. Having done so, you can go on to the practice of tonglen itself, which has four steps.

The first step is very brief. You could think of it as "clearing the decks." You simply allow a little pause, or gap, before you begin. Although this first step is very brief and simple, it is still important. It is like cracking the window to let in a little fresh air.

In the second step, you touch in with the world of feelings and emotions. Each time you breathe in, you breathe in heavy, dark, claustrophobic energy; and each time you breathe out, you breathe out light, refreshing, clear, cool energy. With each breath, the practice shifts direction, so there is an ongoing rhythm back and forth. You are taking the habit of grasping and rejecting and you are reversing it.

The third and fourth steps take that same approach and apply it to specific topics. Start as close to home as possible, with something that actually affects you personally. You should work with a topic that arouses real feelings, something that actually touches you or feels a little raw. It does not need to be anything monumental; it could be quite ordinary. For instance, maybe someone screamed at you when you were driving to work. You could breathe in the aggression they threw at you, and you could breathe out to that person a wish to free them from the pain of that anger. If you yourself have just come down with a sickness, you could breathe in that sickness and breathe out your feeling of health and well-being. The point is to start with something that has some reality or juice in your life.

Once you are underway, it is good to let the practice develop on its own and see where it takes you. In this case, no matter what comes up in your mind, you breathe in what you do not like and you breathe out what you do, or you breathe in what is not so good and breathe out being free of that. For instance, after you breathe in that driver's aggression and breathe out your soothing of that anger, what might come up next is your own anger at being so abused first thing in the morning when you had started out in a pretty good mood. You could breathe that anger in and breathe out the ability not to take such attacks so personally. In that way, your thoughts follow along naturally, revealing more and more subtle layers of grasping and rejecting.

In the fourth step, you expand the practice beyond your own immediate feelings and concerns of the moment. For instance, if you are worried about your friend, you expand that concern to include all the other people now and in the past who have had similar worries. You include everybody who has suffered the pain of seeing someone they are close to in danger or trouble. You breathe in all those worries and breathe out to all those countless beings your wish that they be freed from such pain.

Tonglen practice is a radical departure from our usual way of going about things. It may seem threatening, and even crazy; but it strikes at a very core point: how we barricade ourselves from pain and lose our connection with one another. The irony is that the barricades we create do not help all that much; they just make things worse. We end up more fearful, less willing to extend ourselves, and stunted in our ability to express any true kindness. Tonglen pokes holes in those barricades that we create.

Tonglen is always about connection: making a genuine connection with ourselves and others. It is a practice that draws us out beyond our own concerns to an appreciation that no matter what we happen to be going through, others too have gone through experiences just as intense. In tonglen we are continually expanding our perspective beyond our small, self-preoccupied world. The less we restrict our world, the more of it we can take in—and at the same time, we find that we also have much more to give.

ACHARYA JUDITH LIEF

Judith Lief is a Buddhist teacher and author. She was empowered as a teacher by Chögyam Trungpa Rinpoche and received the title of "Acharya," or senior teacher, from his son, the current head of the Shambhala Buddhist lineage, Sakyong Mipham Rinpoche. Judy has edited many of Chögyam Trungpa's books, both for Shambhala Publications and Vajradhatu Publications. From 1980 to 1985 she served as the Dean of Naropa University in Boulder, Colorado. Judy is also a writer and has written for many publications, including the *Shambhala Sun, Tricycle,* and *O Magazine.* She is the author of *Making Friends with Death: A Buddhist Guide to Encountering Mortality.* Judy travels and teaches extensively. She lives in Yonkers, New York, with her husband, Chuck, the president of Greyston Foundation, and her dog, Jasper.

healing

BY TULKU THONDUP

True healing or well-being is having peace and joy in our lives. The source of this healing is none other than our own mind. The mind is innately peaceful and joyful. Also, peace and joy are concepts created by the mind and experiences felt by the mind. So the most effective way to heal is to use the mind—the right means and the source of meditation.

Although the mind is the source of healing, positive mental objects such as peaceful images have an important role, too. They enable us to tap into our mind's healing powers. For ordinary people like us—who function and sustain ourselves entirely on mental objects created by our habitual dualistic concepts, passions, sen-

sations, and emotions—creating positive images is a powerful inspiration that inevitably leads to true healing.

When we see a mental object, our mind grasps at it as a real, truly existing entity. Once it grasps at an object, the mind starts a process of discrimination, classifying the object as mine or yours, as good or bad, as an object it likes or doesn't like, etc. This enflames the emotional passions of wanting or not wanting, craving or hating. Such emotions bring feelings of sadness or excitement, pain or pleasure. The more intense our feelings and emotions, the tighter our mental grip of grasping. We lose our own birthright, the peaceful center within us, and become slaves of our mental objects, dependent upon external circumstances.

Through meditation, we can realize the awareness of the peaceful and joyful nature of our mind. From there we can interact with mental objects with greater peace and ease on our own terms, from a position of mental strength. Gradually, the tightness of the grip of our grasping loosens, and mental objects transform into the four healing powers, the source of peace and joy.

If our mind is in peace, our emotions will be calm, the four elements of our body will be balanced, and the body's flow of energy circulation will be normal. Our relationships with others will be healthy and beneficial since whatever we say will be the words of peace. Our body's every expression will transmit peace.

In order to find and employ the healing power of our mind and the healing qualities of our mental objects, we must consistently and repeatedly meditate on the four healing powers: positive images, positive words, positive feeling, and positive belief.

Positive images: This is about seeing or visualizing images that we appreciate as a form with positive qualities. Most of the time, our minds are occupied with negative or neutral images. But if we build a habit of seeing or visualizing positive images, then these positive mental objects could awaken the peaceful and joyful nature of our mind spontaneously. Almost all of us, whenever we think, form mental images of whatever we are thinking. The positive and negative qualities of our images invoke and feed joyful or painful concepts, emotions, and feelings in us all the time.

So if we could get into the habit of seeing or visualizing images of religious significance or secular images that have a positive significance, such as a blossoming flower, we would use these images as a powerful source of healing to transform our minds and bodies.

Positive words: This is about thinking of or labeling our positive images with positive words. Positive images can become an even greater source of healing when we empower and magnify them with positive designations. Words or labeling are an integral part of formulating our thoughts. Whenever we think, commentaries, dialogues, and monologues are constantly running through our heads.

So, designate a positive image with a religious prayer or a secular word of positive significance such as "This is a totally beautiful flower." "It is colorful and blossoming." "How wonderful it is!" Repeating the positive words that amplify the positive qualities of the images magnifies their power to heal.

Positive feeling: This is about feeling the qualities of the positive objects mentally and physically. Letting ourselves really feel positive qualities heightens the force of healing. It goes beyond seeing and thinking of the positive object as inspiring. For example, by feeling the freshness, purity, and blossoming attributes of a flower within us, we take those qualities into a deep level of our mind and body.

Positive belief: This is about trusting in the healing power of meditating on positive images, words, and feeling. The point is not to develop blind faith, but to develop an experience of total comfort with the meditative experience that we are doing based upon our own gradual progress in the meditation. Developing unconditioned trust in healing fulfills the healing power of meditation.

The healing meditation here is based on Buddhism. Many Buddhist meditations are unique trainings specifically for Buddhists. But a greater part of its teachings are universal and beneficial to anyone eager to apply them. The meditative methods given here are those open for people of any faith, if their faith permits.

You should start the meditation by bringing the mind back to the body in an atmosphere of peace and calmness. Sit still in a quiet place, closing your eyes, and breathing naturally.

Visualize a totally pure, open, and boundless sky in front of you. Think about and feel the quality of that sky. It brings a sense of clarity and openness, the quality of the sky in you.

Then in that open sky, visualize the image of the Blessed One, the Divine Presence. Many religions believe that the Blessed One is universal. It is within us and outside of us.

However, for people who are used to being conceptual, dualistic, and having their needs fulfilled by higher sources, it is important to meditate and pray to the presence of a higher power as a source of healing. The higher source or Blessed One could be the Buddha, a saint, or a master—if your faith allows. See, think, feel, and believe that this presence is the embodiment of omniscient wisdom, unconditioned love, and all-pervading power from the bottom of your heart.

Then channel the energy of your devotion in the form of prayer to invoke the compassionate blessings of the Blessed One. It is not just words, but the joyful sound of your mind and celebratory feeling of your heart joined by the sound of devotional power of the whole universe. Prayer could be any prayer, positive word, mantra, or just the sacred syllable "Ah." "Ah" has a universal and open quality. According to Buddhism, it is the most

through meditation, we can realize
the awareness of the peaceful and
joyful nature of our mind.

profound word, the source and essence of all expressions.

As the result of prayer, think that blessings are coming toward you in the form of rainbow light-like beams. They merge into you. These lights are immaculate and have the qualities of all four elements —strength of earth, fluidity of water, heat of fire, and mobility of air. These beams are filled with the feelings of bliss and heat—blissful heat—the healing energies.

Think and feel that every cell of your body—from the top of your head to the soles of your feet—is filled with healing light, with healing energies. Its mere touch purifies and heals all the ills of your body and mind. Your body is transformed into a body of healing light with healing energies. Your mind is transformed into a mind of peace and joy. Your breathing becomes waves of healing energies and healing sounds that travel along the cells of your body.

From the Blessed One, the healing light with healing energies extends in all directions, healing every being and the entire universe. All of existence becomes a world of healing light with healing energies.

Finally, recognize and acknowledge whatever positive experience you felt as a result of the meditation. Then let your mind be one with that particular experience, as if you have merged with it, like water pouring into water. Relax without thinking. Do this again and again. This helps bring the healing result to a deeper level of your consciousness and preserve it better.

Early morning is generally the best time to meditate, as your mind could still be in peace and your energy still calm. The best place is a solitary place. Whatever you pick, you should chose the best time and place that you can afford and feel good about. At the beginning, you should meditate for about an hour. Once you feel that you are well-rooted in the meditation, even 5 minutes a day will be a great source of well-being.

Like food, exercise, rest, and medicine, meditation is a very important component of healing and keeping healthy. Healing light dispels all mental and emotional darkness. Healing energies melt mental and physical tumors. Healing meditation loosens the tightness of the mental grip of grasping. It generates the strength of peace and joy. It balances the physical elements and normalizes the flow of circulation. It will not only ease the ills of your body and mind but also heal them from their roots—past mental and emotional tendencies. Once you are healthy, you can share the same with others.

TULKU THONDUP

Tulku Thondup is a widely renowned Lama in the Heart Essence of the Vast Expanse tradition and the author of numerous Buddhist books and translations.

Recognized as the reincarnation of the great Dzogchen Abbot Lushul Khenpo, he has taught at Harvard University and resides in Cambridge, Massachusetts. Sogyal Rinpoche calls his work "priceless." Andrew Weil, M.D., says, "Doctors and patients alike can use his work to promote health and healing."

yoga

BY CYNDI LEE

Opening Poses

In the OM yoga mini-program on this CD, you will be doing a short sequence of yoga asanas (postures) that are coordinated with a breathing pattern. This method of flowing yoga is called Vinyasa Yoga and is a technique for moving our bodies through space—which is what we do all day anyway, except usually without much awareness. I've included drawings to help you learn the poses. As you listen to the CD, keep these drawings in front of you for reference.

This warm-up vinyasa is designed to prepare you specifically for sitting meditation. It will open your shoulders and hips, massage your back muscles, nourish your spine, and expand your lung capacity allowing you to breathe deeply and more efficiently.

Yoga begins to wake us up, first, to our own body. It invites us to move our breath into all the nooks and crannies of that body and to let our mind ride on the breath so that we begin to get quite famil-

iar with ourselves from the inside out. This personal encounter quite naturally leads us back out, and we start to take notice of other people in our world. We might begin to recognize that the way we relate to our own body—fearful, aggressive, gentle, impatient, curious—is similar to how we relate to our friends, co-workers, families, and even strangers.

This awakening, blended with the beneficial habits of breathing deeply and moving gracefully, can begin to give us confidence, clarity, strength, and flexibility in both our muscles and our mind. This balance is called yoga. The word yoga comes from the Sanskrit word *yuj*, which means to yoke or to bind. So even in a brief yoga practice, we can feel our body, breath, and mind joining back together. This sense of reconnection naturally expands to become an experience of reunion with all that is.

The viewpoint of the Buddhist mindfulness and compassion teachings are in harmony with the foundation of traditional yoga, which is *ahimsa*, or "nonharming." So as you sit on your cushion to begin your warm-up vinyasa, see if you can relax your expectations of what you think should happen, what you are supposed to feel, how tight or weak you are, and of how much you really don't like doing exercise even though you know it's good for you. Watch how and where your breath moves through your body. Isn't it amazing?

Don't worry about what you can and can't do. You *can* pay attention, so just stick with that and let everything else that happens be a surprise. Your yoga practice will be different every day, and those nuances will turn out to be more interesting than any agenda you could cook up. So just keep watching your breath going in and going out, feeling what you feel, and rest with that.

The breathing exercises we begin with

are part of a practice called *pranayama*. Pranayama is made up of two words: *prana* and *ayama*. Prana refers to our life force, that mysterious essence that is also found in sunlight, water, and earth. The ancient yogis said that each person is allotted a certain number of breaths in a lifetime, so they suggested that we lengthen each breath in order to extend our lifespan. Ayama means extension; therefore, pranayama means extension of the life force that is already within us. It is a system of manipulated breathing techniques that have many benefits, including cleansing your sinuses, bringing more oxygen to your entire body, and soothing your nervous system.

The breath is considered the link between mind and body. In yoga asana practice as well as pranayama and meditation, we use the breath as a reference point for returning to and resting in the present moment.

If you breathe slowly and deeply, in and out through your nose, you will begin to create a healthy physical environment for your mind to feel restful, your body to be effective, and for the harmonious balance between the two to extend from your practice into your everyday life situations. Hopefully, doing these breathing exercises will come in handy when you are stuck in traffic, confronted by an angry shopper, in charge of the Boy Scouts troop, getting proposed to, having insomnia, or simply sitting on your front porch on a summer's evening.

All you will need to organize your own yoga set-up at home is a clear area about 10 feet × 6 feet. If you have enough space, it's fun to do yoga with a pal. A wooden floor is best, but use whatever you've got. Bare feet are recommended, but if you prefer to keep your socks on, that's okay. When you sit on the floor, it will be helpful to have a couple of cush-

warm-up part 2

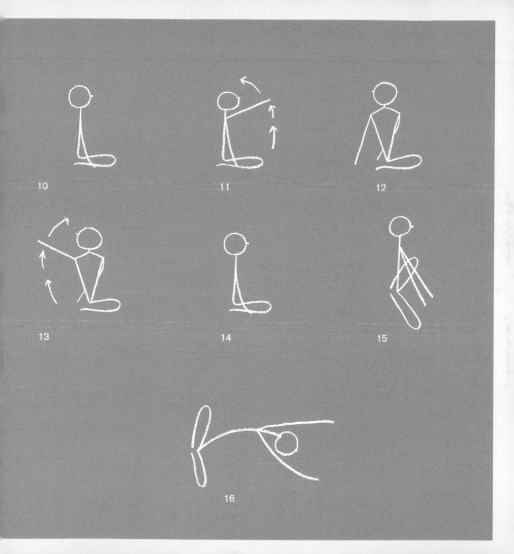

ions to sit on. You can also do most of the warm-up vinyasa in a chair, especially if you are going to do your meditation practice in a chair. Try to follow my instructions, but if you need to modify them, please do, and if you can't do everything, take a rest and then pick up the sequence when you are ready.

One important note regarding yoga and other forms of physical activity you may have tried: Yoga is not a "no pain, no gain" experience. It is in the "no pain, no pain" category. If something hurts when you are doing your yoga practice, then stop and take a break. Discriminate between actual pain and interesting sensation. If you haven't used your body for a while, or ever, you will begin to feel a lot of new things. That might be intense, irritating, or daunting (and of course, it might feel good!), but try to stay with that and watch how it changes over time as your body unfolds.

Please take the approach of ahimsa, "non-harming," as the ground of your yoga. All you need to remember is to keep your breath full, pay attention to what you are feeling, and respond appropriately. Take this opportunity to be kind to yourself.

Another way to be kind to yourself with yoga is to make sure you don't do it on a full stomach. Try to practice at least 2 hours after you have eaten. A nice time to practice is first thing in the morning, but whenever you can find the time is good. The warm-up vinyasa takes less than 5 minutes and is not only a great preparation for meditation but also a great thing to do as a midafternoon break at work instead of a cup of coffee or a cigarette. It is a great pick-me-up after work before going on to your next activity. Even practicing before going to bed at night is nice. Just do what you can, whenever you can, and enjoy making your own acquaintance in this way.

Closing Poses

Savasana is an extremely restorative yoga pose, considered to be one of the most important parts of yoga practice and a good way to end sitting meditation practice. Savasana actually helps us integrate the fruits of our practices. Now, instead of doing yoga, this is when we let the yoga do us. This is a big step for many of us who are not used to doing nothing without falling asleep. But, unfortunately, you may have noticed that sometimes sleep isn't all that restful. How many times have you woke up feeling exhausted?

In the warm-up vinyasa you were asked to feel your sitting bones reaching down into the earth as you extend your fingertips up to the sky, or to drop your head and your tailbone toward each other and then the reverse, extending that energy out from your center. Asana practice is always a multi-directional situation, a physical manifestation of non-duality.

This approach applies to savasana as well. If you look at a picture of someone doing savasana, at first it will look like they are sleeping. But then you will begin to notice how their energy is flowing, bright, yet soft. Savasana means "corpse pose," and the work here is to let go of your physical body but stay mentally aware. The oppositional dynamic of savasana is to be receptive instead of active. Not passive, but receptive. This approach balances our feminine and masculine aspects of outgo and input, form and space, acting and receiving, and generates a state of well-being and wholeness. Because of this, a 5-minute savasana can be much more rejuvenating than a 30-minute nap.

We begin by establishing an environment supportive to physical and mental relaxation through the use of blankets and cushions. You will need a warm, quiet place without too much light. Place a rolled up blanket or a pillow under your knees, especially if you have any discomfort in your lower back. Place a small pillow under your neck and head, an eye pillow or scarf over your eyes, and cover yourself with a blanket. If your floor is cold, put a blanket under you as well.

You can do this guided savasana whenever you have a chance. On the CD it is only 5 minutes long, but please feel free to remain in savasana as long as you like.

Follow my instructions on the CD for how to organize your body on the floor. Placing your body in the correct position is like creating a map for the internal rivers of blood, breath, water, and energy to flow, which will nourish your abdominal organs, rest your muscles, and balance your hormones as well as soothe the nervous system, which, in turn, calms the mind.

As your body is being reprogrammed to reduce brain arousal, fluid retention, adrenal burnout, and toxic buildup, your mind is being invited to watch the process. Letting go of what you want from this practice or from anything else you do is a huge step toward feeling relaxed, restored, rejuvenated. Rather than accomplishing only one goal, this approach provides endless possibility for opening to occur in every level of your being.

CYNDI LEE

Cyndi Lee, founder of New York's OM yoga center, is a practitioner of both hatha yoga and Tibetan Buddhism and has been teaching yoga for over 20 years. OM yoga offers the immediacy of the hatha yoga experience informed by the Buddhist teachings of mindfulness, wisdom, and compassion. Cyndi's background includes studies with many well-known yoga teachers such as Rodney Yee, Judith Lasater, and Sharon Gannon. Her yoga practice and teaching have been most profoundly influenced by her Buddhist teachers, especially Rimpoche Nwagang Gelek and Chögyam Trungpa Rimpoche.

STEVE GORN

Steve Gorn has performed Indian classical music and new American music on the bansuri bamboo flute in concerts and festivals throughout the world. He has recorded and performed with Paul Simon, Krishna Das, Glen Velez, Jack DeJohnette, Paul Winter, Layne Redmond, and others. Steve journeys to India each year to study and perform in a variety of concerts and festivals.

resources

To learn more about Shamatha and Sakyong Mipham Rinpoche's work:

Gampo Abbey
Pleasant Bay
Cape Breton, Nova Scotia
Canada
B0E 2P0
(902) 224-2752
www.gampoabbey.org

Karmê Chöling
369 Patneaude Lane
Barnet, VT 05821
(802) 633-2384
www.kcl.shambhala.org

Rocky Mountain
Shambhala Center
4921 County Road 68C
Red Feather Lakes, CO 80545
(970) 881-2184
www.rmsc.shambhala.org

Shambhala International
1084 Tower Road
Halifax, Nova Scotia
Canada
B3H 2Y5
(902) 420-1118
www.shambhala.org

To learn more about Vipassana and Larry Rosenberg's work:

Abhayagiri Buddhist Monastery
16201 Tomki Road
Redwood Valley, CA 95470
(707) 485-1630
www.abhayagiri.org

Barre Center for
Buddhist Studies
149 Lockwood Road
Barre, MA 01005
(978) 355-2347
www.dharma.org

Bhāvanā Society
Route 1, Box 218-3
High View, WV 26808
(304) 856-3241
www.bhavanasociety.org

Cambridge Insight
Meditation Center
331 Broadway
Cambridge, MA 02139
(617) 441-9038
http://world.std.com/~cimc

Insight Meditation Society
1230 Pleasant Street
Barre, MA 01005
(978) 355-4378
www.dharma.org

Spirit Rock Meditation Center
P.O. Box 909
5000 Sir Francis Drake
Boulevard
Woodacre, CA 94973
(415) 488-0164
www.spiritrock.org

Books by Larry Rosenberg:

Breath by Breath: The Liberating Practice of Insight Meditation
(Shambhala Publications)

Living in the Light of Death: On the Art of Being Truly Alive
(Shambhala Publications)

To learn more about Zen and Edward Espe Brown's work:

Green Gulch Farm Zen Center
1601 Shoreline Highway
Sausalito, CA 94965
(415) 383-3134

San Francisco Zen Center
300 Page Street
San Francisco, CA 94102
(415) 863-3136
www.sfzc.com

Tassajara
39171 Tassajara Road
Carmel Valley, CA 93924
(831) 659-2229

Books Written or Edited by Edward Espe Brown:

The Greens Cookbook: Extraordinary Vegetarian Cuisine from the Celebrated Restaurant
by Deborah Madison with Edward Espe Brown
(Broadway Books)

Not Always So: Talks on the True Spirit of Zen
by Shunryu Suzuki
(HarperCollins)

The Tassajara Bread Book
(Shambhala Publications)

Tomato Blessings and Radish Teachings: Recipes and Reflections
(Riverhead Books)

To learn more about Metta and Sharon Salzberg's work:

Insight Meditation Society
1230 Pleasant Street
Barre, MA 01005
(978) 355-4378
www.dharma.org

Barre Center for Buddhist Studies
149 Lockwood Road
Barre, MA 01005
(978) 355-2347
www.dharma.org

Books and Audio Cassettes by Sharon Salzberg:

A Heart as Wide as the World: Stories on the Path of Lovingkindness
(Shambhala Publications)

Loving-kindness: The Revolutionary Art of Happiness
(Shambhala Publications)

*Loving-Kindness Meditation:
Learning to Love through
Insight Meditation*
(Sounds True)

*Voices of Insight: Teachers of
Buddhism in the West Share
Their Wisdom, Stories, and
Experiences of Insight
Meditation*
(Shambhala Publication)

**To learn more about Tonglen
and Judith Lief's work:**

Gampo Abbey
Pleasant Bay
Cape Breton, Nova Scotia
Canada
B0E 2P0
(902) 224-2752
www.gampoabbey.org

Naropa University
2130 Arapahoe Avenue
Boulder, CO 80302
(303) 444-0202
www.naropa.edu

Shambhala International
1084 Tower Road
Halifax, Nova Scotia
Canada
B3H 2Y5
(902) 420-1118
www.shambhala.org

Books Written or Edited
by Judith Lief:

*Making Friends with Death:
A Buddhist Guide to
Encountering Mortality*
(Shambhala Publications)

Dharma Art by Chögyam
Trungpa Rinpoche
(Shambhala Publications)

*The Art of Calligraphy: Joining
Heaven and Earth* by
Chögyam Trungpa Rinpoche
(Shambhala Publications)

The Heart of the Buddha by
Chögyam Trungpa Rinpoche
(Shambhala Publications)

*Training the Mind and
Cultivating Loving-Kindness*
by Chögyam Trungpa Rinpoche
(Shambhala Publications)

**To learn more about Healing
Meditation and Tulku
Thondup's work**, please visit
www.tulkuthondup.com

Books by Tulku Thondup:

*Boundless Healing: Meditation
Exercises to Enlighten the Mind
and Heal the Body*
(Shambhala Publications)

Enlightened Journey: Buddhist Practice as Daily Life
(Shambhala Publications)

Hidden Teachings of Tibet: An Explanation of the Terma Tradition of Tibetan Buddhism
(Wisdom Publications)

Masters of Meditation and Miracles: Lives of the Great Buddhist Masters of India and Tibet
(Shambhala Publications)

The Healing Power of Mind: Simple Meditation Exercises for Health, Well-Being, and Enlightenment
(Shambhala Publications)

To learn more about OM yoga and Cyndi Lee's work, please visit www.omyoga.com.

Books and CDs by Cyndi Lee:

OM Yoga in a Box (Basic Level) (Hay House)

OM Yoga in a Box for Couples
(Hay House)

OM Yoga in a Box: Intermediate Level
(Hay House)

OM Yoga: A Guide to Daily Practice
(Chronicle Books)

Yoga Body, Buddha Mind
(Riverhead)

For more information on Steve Gorn's luminous music, please visit www.stevegorn.com

Steve Gorn's discography:

Bansuri Bamboo Flute: Indian Ragas
(Music of the World)

Colors of the Mind
(Dharma Moon)

Drala (with David Nichtern)
(Dharma Moon)

Midnight Flower (with David Nichtern)
(Dharma Moon)

Parampara (with Samir Chaterjee)
(Welt Musik)

Pranam
(Biswas)

Wings and Shadows
(with Warren Senders)
(Bamboo Ras)

Steve Gorn is a Dharma
Moon recording artist:
www.dharmamoon.com

Other Resources:
Magazines and Books

Shambhala Sun
The *Shambhala Sun* is the
magazine about waking up,
bringing a Buddhist view to all
the important issues of modern
life. www.shambhalasun.com

Tricycle
Tricycle is a nonprofit quarterly
magazine with an educational
charter to spread the dharma.
www.tricycle.com

Shambhala Publications
Shambhala publishes serious
books of lasting value that
separate the real from the hype.
www.shambhala.com

Sounds True
Audio, video, music for
the inner life.
www.soundstrue.com

Wisdom Publications
Buddhist books for
the benefit of all.
www.wisdompubs.org

Meditation Supplies

DharmaCrafts
www.dharmacrafts.com

Samadhi Cushions
www.samadhicushions.com

credits

CD One: Meditations

1. Welcome   :56

2. Shamatha   7:49
   Sakyong Mipham Rinpoche

3. Vipassana   8:56
   Larry Rosenberg

4. Zazen   10:33
   Edward Espe Brown

5. Metta   11:53
   Sharon Salzberg

6. Tonglen   12:17
   Acharya Judith Lief

7. Healing   11:00
   Tulku Thondup

8. Opening Yoga Poses   9:00
   Cyndi Lee

9. Closing Yoga Poses   5:01
   Cyndi Lee

Produced by Susan Piver,
Padma Projects,
www.padmaprojects.com

Edited and Mastered
by Rick Rowe, MediaForce,
New York, NY

**CD Two: Music for
Contemplation**

Luminous Ragas

Steve Gorn,
Bansuri Flute

Mark Levinson,
Tamboura

1. Rag Shivaranjani   12:35

2. Rag Desh   9:19

3. Rag Chandrakauns   22:17

All compositions by
Steve Gorn, Bamboo Ras, BMI

"The three pieces on this
recording are all evening or late
night ragas. They have the quality of light shining through
darkness, glowing, effervescent."
—Steve Gorn

Judith Lief essay excerpted from
*Making Friends with Death: A Buddhist
Guide to Encountering Mortality* © 2001.
Reprinted by arrangement with
Shambhala Publications, Inc.

Sharon Salzberg essay excerpted from
Insight Meditation © 2001.
Reprinted by arrangement with
Sounds True.

dedication of merit

We close meditation by dedicating any good that may have arisen from our practice to the benefit of others. This way, you are practicing for the whole world, not just for yourself. (Thank you.)

You may use any words you like to indicate your intention to practice for the benefit of all beings, or you may recite these, a Jewel Heart Sangha translation of *The Four Immeasurables*:

may all beings have happiness and
causes of happiness.
may all beings be free from suffering
and the causes of suffering.
may all beings never be parted
from freedom's true joy.
may all beings dwell in equanimity,
free from attachment and aversion.